EDGE
BOOKS™

HOW TO DRAW
GRIFFINS, UNICORNS,
AND OTHER MYTHICAL BEASTS

BY A.J. SAUTTER
FEATURING 5 ARTISTS

CAPSTONE PRESS
a capstone imprint

Edge Books are published by Capstone Press,
1710 Roe Crest Drive, North Mankato, Minnesota 56003
www.mycapstone.com

Library of Congress Cataloging-in-Publication Data
Sautter, Aaron, author.
How to draw griffins, unicorns, and other mythical beasts / by A.J. Sautter.
pages cm.—(Edge Books. Drawing Fantasy Creatures)
Includes bibliographical references.
Summary: "Simple, step-by-step instructions teach readers how to draw griffins, unicorns,
minotaurs, and several other mythical creatures"—Provided by publisher.
ISBN 978-1-4914-8025-0 (library binding)
ISBN 978-1-4914-8409-8 (eBook PDF)
1. Fantasy in art—Juvenile literature. 2. Animals, Mythical, in art—Juvenile literature.
3. Drawing—Technique—Juvenile literature. I. Title.
NC825.F25S28 2016
743'.87—dc23   2015026182

Editorial Credits
Kyle Grenz, designer; Kelly Garvin, media researcher; Gene Bentdahl, production specialist

Illustration Credits
Capstone Press: Colin Howard, cover, 1, 14-15, 16-17, 26-27, Jason Juta, back cover, 18-19,
22-23, 28-31, Martin Bustamante, cover, 1, 6-7, 8-9, 10-11, 12-13, Stefano Azzalin, cover, 1,
20-21, 24-25

Design Elements
Capstone Press; Shutterstock: aopsan, Bambuh, blue pencil, Kompaniets, Marta Jonina,
Molodec, val lawless

TABLE OF CONTENTS

DRAWING MYTHICAL BEASTS

Most fantasy worlds are amazing and magical places. But they are often filled with danger. Heroes in fantastic tales sometimes meet friendly creatures such as griffins or unicorns. But they often encounter minotaurs, harpies, and other deadly monsters as well.

Beasts such as these live only in myths, legends, and fantastic tales. But with a little imagination, these creatures can come alive on paper. Perhaps you enjoy sketching your favorite mythical creatures. If that's true, then this book is for you! Just follow the drawing steps to begin sketching sea serpents, gorgons, chimeras, and other legendary beasts. After practicing them a few times, you can try drawing them in new settings and situations. Then when your art is ready, you can color it using colored pencils, markers, or paints. Are you ready to set your inner artist free? Let's get started!

FINDING YOUR STYLE

Don't worry if your drawings aren't exactly like those you see in this book. Every artist has his or her own style. If you keep practicing, your own art style will develop over time. Soon you'll be creating awesome creatures and fantasy artwork of your very own.

GATHER YOUR SUPPLIES

Before you can start drawing, you'll need to gather some basic supplies. With the following materials in hand, you'll be ready to sketch anything your imagination can create.

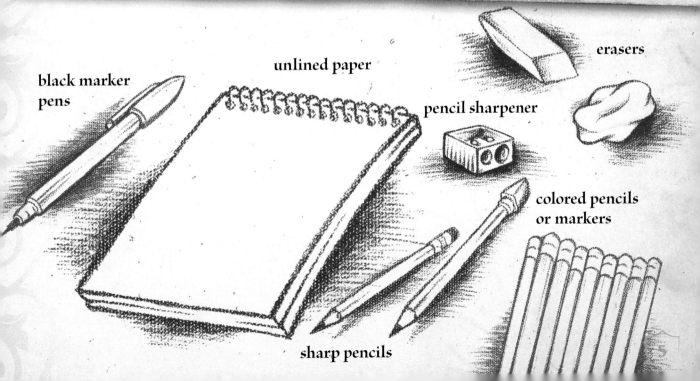

black marker pens

unlined paper

erasers

pencil sharpener

colored pencils or markers

sharp pencils

GRIFFINS

Griffins usually live alone and spend much of their time hunting for food. They can track prey over long distances. Occasionally they will hunt in small packs to trap and kill large prey. A few griffins are friendly toward people and may offer help to those in need.

SIZE: 7 TO 7.5 FEET (2.1 TO 2.3 METERS) LONG; WINGSPAN UP TO 20 FEET (6 M)

HABITAT: DRY CAVES IN GRASSY HILLS OR MOUNTAIN REGIONS

Physical Features: A griffin's upper body has the head, wings, and razor-sharp talons of a large bird of prey. Its lower body features the powerful legs, claws, and tail of a lion. Griffins are usually covered with a mix of golden hair and feathers. They also have incredible eyesight and can spot a rabbit moving up to 3 miles (5 kilometers) away.

1

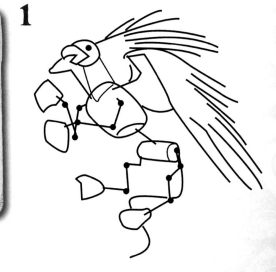

2

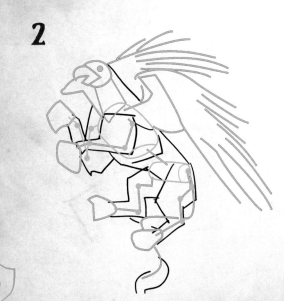

3

FINAL

WHAT'S NEXT?

After drawing this griffin, try drawing it flying into battle to help its human friends

4

5

HARPIES

Harpies are often found perched on rocky cliffs by the sea watching for prey. Harpies will eat almost any kind of meat, but they like human flesh the best. They use their magical singing ability to cloud the minds of human victims and draw them close before attacking. Harpies never bother to bathe themselves. They stink horribly from the bits of rotting filth that covers their feathered bodies.

SIZE: 4 TO 4.5 FEET (1.2 TO 1.4 M) TALL; WINGSPAN UP TO 9 FEET (2.7 M)

HABITAT: ROCKY CLIFFS AND SMALL CAVES NEAR THE SEA

Physical Features: Harpies have the bodies of large birds such as vultures or owls. They have large, powerful wings and strong scaly legs. Their feet are tipped with razor-sharp talons. However, harpies' heads appear as hideous women with yellow eyes, greasy hair, and decaying teeth.

1

2

3

WHAT'S NEXT?

Next try to draw a small flock of harpies perched on a cliff trying to lure a ship of sailors closer to shore with their magical singing.

FINAL

4

5

PHOENIXES

Phoenixes are very private creatures. They prefer to live far from humans. But these mysterious birds are good and noble. They do whatever they can to fight the forces of evil. In rare cases phoenixes have become loyal friends to good wizards. They come to their friends' aid whenever they are called.

SIZE: 10 TO 12 FEET (3 TO 3.7 M) TALL; WINGSPAN UP TO 30 FEET (9 M)

HABITAT: ROCKY CLIFFS IN MOUNTAIN REGIONS

Physical Features: When a phoenix becomes angry, its feathers begin to glow a fiery red color. These powerful magical birds are strong enough to lift and carry an adult elephant. Phoenix tears can magically heal serious wounds in a matter of seconds. Phoenix feathers also have magical properties. Wizards often place them inside their magic wands to make them more powerful.

1

2

3

4

5

WHAT'S NEXT?

Now try drawing this phoenix fighting alongside its wizard friend as they battle an army of wicked orcs and goblins.

FINAL

PEGASI

Pegasi live alone in the wild and are not easily tamed. They are intelligent and do not tolerate evil. They react violently toward wicked people. However, if someone treats a pegasus with respect, it may become a loyal friend. It may even allow that person to ride it into battle.

SIZE: 8 TO 8.5 FEET (2.4 TO 2.6 M) LONG; WINGSPAN UP TO 25 FEET (7.6 M)

HABITAT: FORESTS AND GRASSY PLAINS

Physical Features: Pegasi are very similar to horses. They have powerful bodies, strong legs, muscular necks, and noble faces. Their hair is usually white or light gray. Their powerful wings allow them to fly up to 50 miles (80 km) per hour. Their manes and tails are made of hair and feathers.

1

2

3

WHAT'S NEXT?

After drawing this pegasus, try to draw it flying into battle carrying a human warrior on its back.

FINAL

4

5

UNICORNS

Unicorns are fierce protectors of their forest homes. They do not tolerate evil in any form. They normally live alone or with a mate deep in the forest. Unicorns want nothing to do with humans. But they are often friendly toward elves and other creatures that respect nature.

SIZE: 8 TO 8.5 FEET (2.4 TO 2.6 M) LONG

HABITAT: GRASSY CLEARINGS IN LARGE FORESTS

Physical Features: Unicorns resemble large white horses. However, they usually have bright blue or violet eyes. A unicorn's most famous feature is the 2 to 3 foot (0.6 to 0.9 m) ivory horn that grows from its head. These horns have strong magical properties. They can be used to make strong healing potions. Some wizards even craft unicorn horns into powerful magic wands.

1

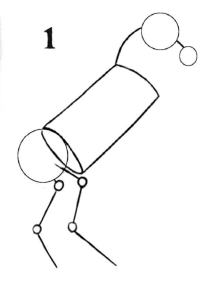

2

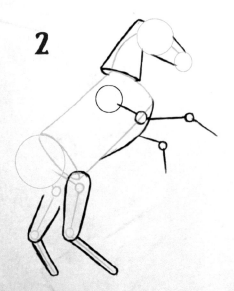

3

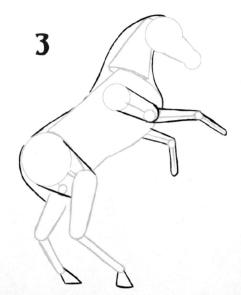

4

5

FINAL

WHAT'S NEXT?

When you're done drawing
this unicorn, try drawing two
of them chasing a wicked
forest troll out of the woods.

MINOTAURS

Minotaurs spend most of their time prowling their mazelike caves for their next meal. They have an amazing sense of direction and never get lost. This ability is a great advantage. It helps minotaurs hunt down humans and other prey that wander into their mazelike homes.

SIZE: 7.5 TO 8 FEET (2.3 TO 2.4 M) TALL

HABITAT: MAZELIKE NETWORKS OF UNDERGROUND CAVES, OR TUNNELS AND SEWERS UNDER ANCIENT CITIES

Physical Features: Minotaurs are a strange combination of humans and bulls. Their heads and lower bodies are like a bull's. But their arms and torsos are similar to a human's. Minotaurs are covered in shaggy black or brown hair and have hooves instead of feet. All minotaurs have sharp, deadly horns used for attacking their enemies and prey.

1

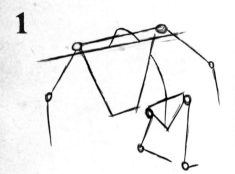

2

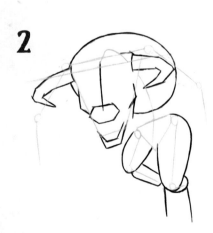

3

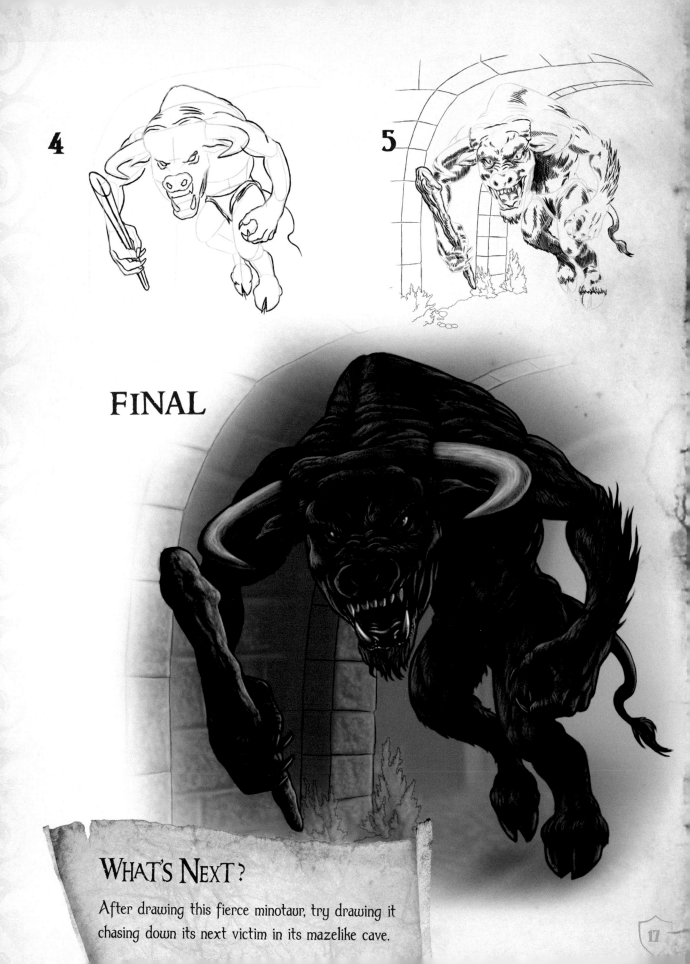

4

5

FINAL

WHAT'S NEXT?

After drawing this fierce minotaur, try drawing it chasing down its next victim in its mazelike cave.

CHIMERAS

Most chimeras are dim-witted beasts. They normally live alone and spend much of their time hunting for food. These creatures are completely loyal to the wicked gods and wizards who created them. If a chimera's creator orders it to attack an enemy, it will do so without question.

SIZE: 6.5 FEET (2 M) TALL; 15 FEET (4.6 M) LONG
HABITAT: DRY CAVES IN HILLY REGIONS

Physical Features: Chimeras are a combination of several creatures. Most have two heads—one of a powerful lion and one of a horned goat. A chimera's tail takes the form of a huge snake with a deadly, poisonous bite. These beasts have front feet resembling a dragon's claws and their hind feet are shaped like a goat's hooves.

1

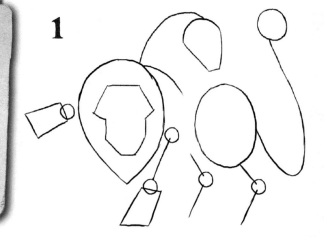

2

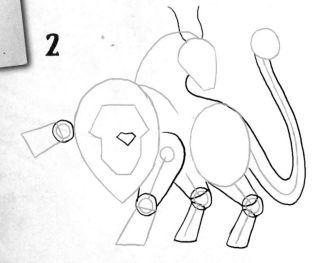

3

4

5

FINAL

WHAT'S NEXT?

After practicing this chimera, try drawing one with different kinds of heads. Give it a tiger's head, a bear's head, or even the head and wings of a dragon!

GORGONS

Gorgons prefer to live by themselves and don't like intruders. Most gorgons are expert shots with bows and arrows. They also have a powerful magical defense. One look from an angry gorgon's glowing eyes will turn an enemy to stone. Gorgon lairs are often filled with statues of those foolish enough to be caught by these wicked creatures.

SIZE: 5 TO 5.5 FEET (1.5 TO 1.7 M) TALL
HABITAT: CAVES AND OLD CASTLES NEAR THE SEA

Physical Features: Most gorgons have lower bodies resembling large snakes. They have rough, scaly skin that is usually green or brown in color. They have jagged teeth, sharp fangs, and a forked tongue. Gorgons are most famous for the nest of squirming snakes they have in place of normal hair.

1

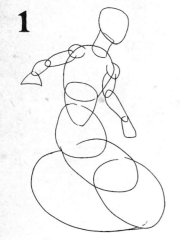

2

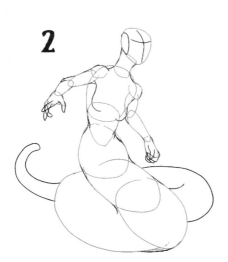

3

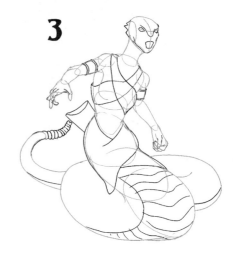

4

5

6

FINAL

WHAT'S NEXT?

Now try drawing another gorgon as she hunts for a new victim inside her ruined castle by the sea.

CERBERUS

Cerberus spends its time wandering rocky plains and lava fields near volcanoes. Nobody knows why it lurks in such locations. It's thought that Cerberus may be guarding a secret entrance to its master's lair. An evil wizard may have raised Cerberus up from the Underworld to be his personal guard dog.

SIZE: 6.5 TO 7 FEET (2 TO 2.1 M) TALL
HABITAT: ROCKY PLAINS AND LAVA FIELDS

Physical Features: Cerberus appears as a huge, three-headed dog. It's covered with short brown and black hair. The beast's feet are tipped with sharp claws, and each of its three mouths is filled with wicked, gnashing teeth. Cerberus can launch large balls of fire from its mouths to overwhelm its victims.

1

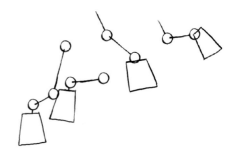

2

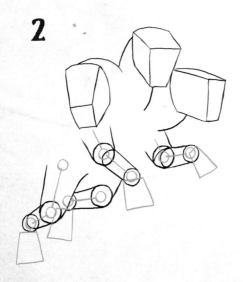

3

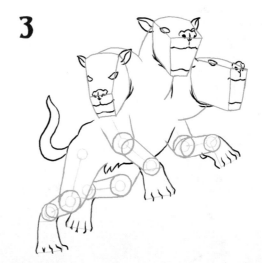

4

5

FINAL

WHAT'S NEXT?

Next try drawing
Cerberus belching out a
huge fireball at a victim
near its volcano home.

23

SEA SERPENTS

Sea serpents spend almost all of their time hunting for food. These creatures normally hunt large prey like whales or giant squid. But they will occasionally attack human ships. They first coil their huge bodies around the ships and crush them. They then eat the sailors who try to jump to safety. Only a few sailors have survived a sea serpent's attack.

SIZE: 150 TO 200 FEET (46 TO 61 M) LONG
HABITAT: WARM OCEAN WATERS

Physical Features: Sea serpents are often called sea dragons because of their dragonlike appearance. Their gigantic snakelike bodies are covered with tough scaly skin. Many sea serpents have dragonlike heads and mouths filled with deadly teeth. Some sea serpents may even have large fins that resemble a dragon's wings.

1

2

3

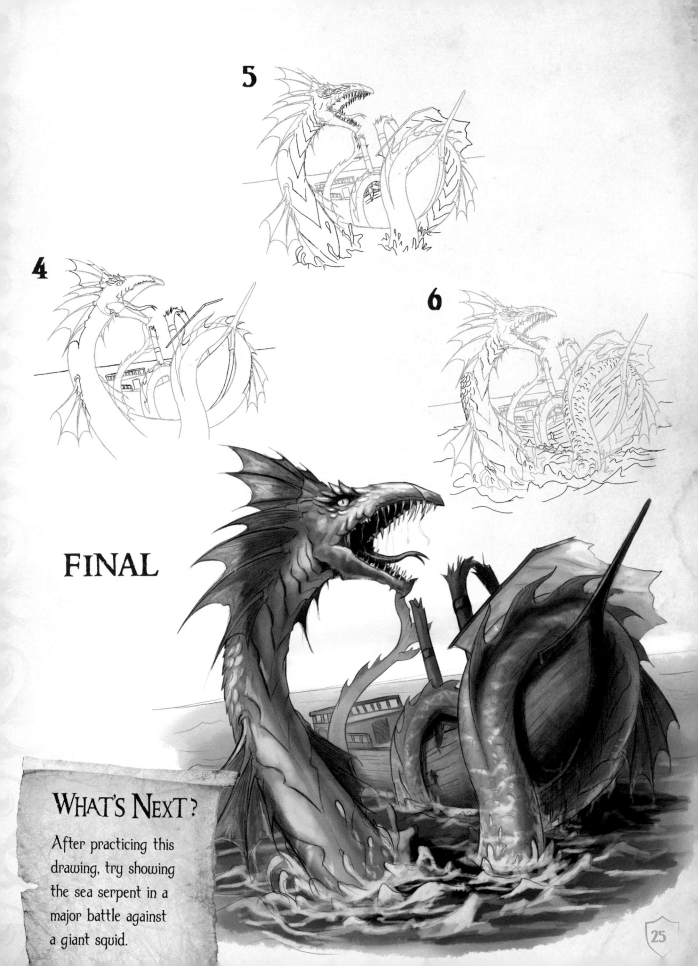

5

4

6

FINAL

WHAT'S NEXT?

After practicing this
drawing, try showing
the sea serpent in a
major battle against
a giant squid.

KRAKENS

Krakens are among the largest and deadliest creatures of any fantasy world. They like attacking ships and enjoy the taste of human flesh. A kraken first wraps its huge tentacles around a ship. It then crushes the ship and pulls it under the water. After sinking the ship, the monster grabs the doomed sailors and stuffs them into its gaping mouth.

SIZE: MORE THAN 350 FEET (107 M) LONG
HABITAT: LARGE CAVES ON THE OCEAN FLOOR

Physical Features: Krakens resemble gigantic squids or octopuses with tough, rubbery skin. Their huge eyes help them find prey in the darkest ocean waters. Krakens are best known for their 10 powerful tentacles. However, their deadly mouths are filled with hundreds of huge, swordlike teeth that can kill prey in an instant.

3

1

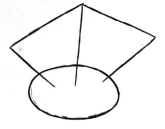

2

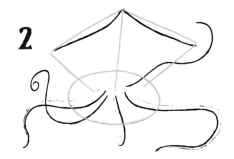

FINAL

4

6

5

WHAT'S NEXT?

When you're done drawing this huge kraken, try a new drawing that shows it attacking a large merchant ship.

CHIMERA vs. CERBERUS

Long ago two evil wizards desired to control the same country. To gain an advantage, one of them created the vicious chimera. He used it to force local villagers to obey his will. Not to be outdone, the second wizard raised Cerberus from the Underworld to even the odds. The two mythical beasts are evenly matched in fierceness and strength. They are locked in a never-ending battle, and nobody can say which one will claim the ultimate victory for its master.

CHIMERA

SIZE: ABOUT 6.5 FEET (2 M) TALL; UP TO 15 FEET (4.6 M) LONG

HABITAT: DRY CAVES IN HILLY REGIONS

CERBERUS

SIZE: 6.5 TO 7 FEET (2 TO 2.1 M) TALL

HABITAT: ROCKY PLAINS AND LAVA FIELDS

1

2

3

4

5

6

7

8

9

When you're finished with this drawing, try adding more mythical beasts to the battle. Do you think the minotaur would fight with the chimera? Will a gorgon join up with Cerberus? The choice is up to you!

FINAL

READ MORE

Beaumont, Steve. *Drawing Unicorns and Other Mythological Beasts.* Drawing Legendary Monsters. New York: PowerKids Press, 2011.

Berry, Bob. *How to Draw Magical, Monstrous & Mythological Creatures.* Irvine, Calif.: Walter Foster Publishing, 2012.

Fiegenschuh, Emily. *The Explorer's Guide to Drawing Fantasy Creatures.* Cincinnati, Ohio: Impact, 2011.

INTERNET SITES

FactHound offers a safe, fun way to find Internet sites related to this book. All of the sites on FactHound have been researched by our staff.

Here's all you do:

Visit *www.facthound.com*

Type in this code: 9781491480250

Super-cool stuff!

Check out projects, games and lots more at
www.capstonekids.com